Why Not Take All of Me

*A Cycle of Poems on the
Life and Music of Billie Holiday*

Joel Peckham

FUTURECYCLE PRESS

www.futurecycle.org

Published by FutureCycle Press
Hayesville, North Carolina, USA

ISBN 978-1-938853-43-2

Contents

Foreword

A short note on this slim volume

I began writing this sequence almost by accident while working on a long poem focused roughly on the question of why so much great art seems to derive out of dissipation. Somewhere within a fairly aimless riff, I found myself contemplating the music and life of Billie Holiday. Not long after I had written the words, "this authentic fraudulence, this art," I knew I had hit on a subject much more complicated and dangerous than what I had started with. I also tried to resist it. Taking on an iconic figure as a subject is replete with many hazards. For one, Billie has been written about many times. As biography and research goes, one cannot do much better, for example, than Donald Clarke's *Wishing on the Moon*—a wonderfully comprehensive and lovingly detailed volume from which all quoted material referenced in this book is derived. And there are other very strong biographies available to anyone curious to find a historically rigorous account of her life, including Stuart Nicholson's excellent *Billie Holiday* and *The Many Faces of Billie Holiday* by Robert O'Meally. For that reason, I have not written a biography in verse.

Although no events have been invented, scenes have been elaborated to develop tone, nuance and tension. And, of course, my own impression of Billie Holiday—taken from my own research and obsession with her music—creates a lens through which the reader will see the author as much as his subject. The effect of Billie Holiday on those around her, and even on this poet, is a part of the story as well. Ultimately, this collection is meant to be a meditation on the life and music of one of the true great artists of the twentieth century—an impressionistic exploration of the connection between personality, identity, celebrity, and art.

Rough edges have been deliberately included here as well as third-rail examinations of sex, race, gender, addiction, and psychological dysfunction. I make no apologies for them, and that is appropriate: Billie Holiday made no apologies for who she was or how she lived. Her life was reflected in her music, especially in the latter part of her career.

She chose and wrote songs that spoke to her and through her and, in her best work, it is nearly impossible to separate the singer from the

music she sang. In these poems I examine Billie Holiday, telling her story while exploring the significance of her art and her myth to American music, history, and culture. Therefore, even though there is a strong element of storytelling in the work, the poems are meant to be lyrical and meditative. They do not take a smoothly linear approach but rather tell her story in a call-and-response fashion, with most poems exploring a theme or subject—love, addiction, family, time, race, tone, melody, sex, identity, etc.—and then exploring the same subject from a slightly different point of view or angle of insight.

In *Why Not Take All of Me,* the voice is fluid, slipping from the poet, to an unnamed audience member, to a fellow musician, and around again. My hope is that a multidimensional portrait will emerge—one that doesn't so much dispel the carefully constructed myth of Billie Holiday (one that she herself nurtured) as examine the relationship between that myth, her life, and her music. I hope I did her some measure of justice. I'd like to think she'd enjoy this little book.

—Joel Peckham

Prologue

1.

She was a prostitute daughter
of reform schools with a voice as thin
as heroin. Even the come-on was
a ragged beauty, torched
and bruised. When the song is right
it makes a strange and bitter fruit.

2.

As if the song were *just* another trick
Billie turned. And how she learned
so much of what she knew by listening to
the moan beneath her as she floated
high above the sweat-damp room.
That growl that trembling tone that
starts up in the chest and rises when
we must approximate desire, love—
this authentic fraudulence, this art.

Billie and the Art of Paraphrase

1.

Sometimes she would linger so far back
behind the beat she could wave
to it from shore, like a girl on the docks:
The Point. Baltimore. Lackadaisical,
laconic, *don't care-ish,* as anyone
whose daddy's gone but still around, playing
rhythm at every bar. Whose mother,
half-gone, waves a gun outside her latest
lover's home. So everyone knows or thinks
they know. So. Maybe she learned to hold back, *just*
—become the prettiest, *evilest* girl at the party,
wait for everyone and everything to come to her.
(And were there ever parties, in the bottoms
in alley apartments where at fourteen
she'd smoke reefers with the pimps and sing
with Louis and Bessie on the Old Victrolas.)
So much must go wrong for you to be so
there and so far off.

2.

Such a practiced indifference to the rhythm
of the band that didn't back her up so much
as wait for her to take a breath,
watch the rise of breast and throat.
Filling in the windows Lester Young
would name it. Still he never knew exactly
when they would lift or fly open or how far
or if and when he blew his horn his *baby'd*
still be in the room or already hustling down
the hall. (He always found her though.) The whole
time, Lady so composed, she recomposed
the song, the notes, even the words. They stretched
and pulled apart. And we did too. *Why not take all
of me* she sang and each time not
the same at *all*.

Billie Turns a Trick

1.

She claimed she liked the white men
best—the regulars who knew just
what they wanted. "When they came
to see me it was wham bang, they gave me
money and were gone. Negroes keep you
up all the damn night, handing you that stuff
about 'Is it good' and 'Don't you want
to be my Old Lady.'"* She was no one's
Lady, but she wore the name lightly
as a slip of silk, something she could
shrug off, like a beam of light, like
a regular. Get him off. Get him out.
Send him away, down the dim-lit
corridors thinking he had known
"colored," had a taste, something he
could take—a dark song singing
made his own.

*All quotations taken from *Billy Holiday: Wishing on the Moon* by Donald Clarke (Cambridge: DaCapo Press, 2002).

2.

Sometimes it's just easier
that way—no desperate fingers
in her hair, no body seething to connect
or like the boy who wept
the whole night long because
he'd have to work a week of
scrubbing hog-parts off linoleum
to pay for her. Or the one who put
his fist two inches in the wall above
her just to make her see him feel
him there. Beneath above behind
you sing in pain and in pain breathe
it down get only what you learn
and earn. You're lucky if you
get paid to sing the song.

Billie Holiday Doesn't Give a Fuck

She just suffered, she got to love suffering
because she didn't know what love was
—Marie Bryant, Jazz singer

1.

Most nights she would start late, one maybe two
hours past the hour when the set was meant
to start, but she was never that on time in life
or art. She made her own time
and by then languid with the heroin... *Just*
a minute she would whisper to the manager,
tap-tapping on the door, and minutes would
slide by. So the band would just get lit
and light, smoke cigarettes, let someone else
chase Lady. You might as well push smoke.
It might be 2 a.m. but even old white women
in their long black skirts would wait for her
until she came on drifting, regal. Just a sheath
of satin with a little shimmer over naked skin,
one white flower in her hair. She would
hang there still and seem to sway.
Lights were hot and blurred. And so
was she. And whoever played the keys that night
—Clyde Hart, Eddie Heywood, Joe Springer (she
always found a good one on piano)—would just
have to start and play, go his way until she felt

like going hers. *My man he don't love me / Treats me ooh so mean.* Her voice would seem to wander around inside the song, the room, gliding up on horn and drums, light palm slid along a cheek bone like a breath of wind or one light finger pressed on lips, an eyelash kiss. Then gone and back. A flirt. A come-on that would leave you checking for your wallet *and* your heart. They all loved Billie, the musicians who might share her bed or not, the big boys and the wispy girls she sometimes pulled into a cab and used to use her. Sex like powder she could cook and smoke. But the song—*Love will make you drink and gamble / Make you stay out all night long*—only Billie seemed to leave the song intact, and she left when she wanted. *Love will make you do things that you know is wrong...* She gave you freedom, taking hers. And still you'd cry when Billie glided out the door.

2.

You want to make her simply tragic and you
fall in love with that idea. That's the first
mistake. Billie, she shakes free of simple.
Yes *every man she ever loved was bad*. But
she liked them bad. Yes she was an addict.
So is everyone. *She was addictive.*

The hustlers and the pimps, they needed
her. Like Jimmy Monroe at the table up front.
*He wears his high trimmed pants / stripes
are really yellow.* Large-as-life, good-looking,
sharply dressed. Could have any girl, but he
needed Billie and not just for the money. Even
when they beat her, it was proof they couldn't
stand that need and couldn't leave. No one
could. *But when he starts to love me, he's so fine
and mellow.* Listen to her nonchalance
that isn't quite. Ride with her in the cab
between the sets each night.
Share the reefer on her fingertips and laugh
her laugh. Sometimes she would take a guy
backstage to work out an arrangement and she'd
be standing in the middle of the room in high-heels
and a pair of earrings. That's it. She'd go
through the entire song like that, and the poor
kid wouldn't know where to look or if he could

and if he tried to leave it was, "Where you think
you goin *motherfucker*." Voice the echo of a high-
pitched bell. On wind. There is no strike, just

the sound. From nowhere floating pure
and impure, always in transition. She could
call you *motherfucker* and you feel almost
blessed. And even in a single octave (which is all
she ever had and sometimes less on a cold
night) so much nuance bending over rooftops

swimming the river out to sea and back, bouncing
off the awnings and the concrete, riding
moonlight. Listen. *Love is like a faucet / It turns
off and on.* When she bends that note
up just a little so its wrong and right—*Sometimes
when you think it's on.* Like half a smile.
Wicked. *Baby.* Right there. *It's turned off
and gone.* That's Billie, having the time of her life.

The Lady and the President

It was like brother and sister, but another thing.
He was so strange. He was like a visitor.
And she was too.
—Jimmy Rowles, Jazz Pianist

1. The President Makes an Appearance

He came on easy, the way
light wind pushes on a door and you just feel it
in the room. Look up and he's there slouching
on the bandstand watching Lady Day, his Lady,
take her place to slip and slide her way through
"Billie's Blues." Swooping in and falling down, with
her little growl. *Some people say I'm built*
for speed, she purrs and stares right through
the man she named her Prez. Lester, making
"nice eyes," porkpie sitting low, horn across
his lap and waiting for a turn—an invitation
he had written for himself. Whoever she had
playing horn would slide back. He's the president
and everybody knows. Willis Lester Young
never did impose. But slid in from the melody,
smooth and rolling, moving like a searchlight
over dark waves, testing the waters playing
with the mist. And when the other players
teased him for that gentleness, he'd tap
his head and say, "You boys are all belly. Me,
I got things going on—up here."

2. The President Plays it Cool

He had a language all his own—
a way of making nonsense sense. *Bread*
for money. *Deep* to name a heavy thing like
thought or pain. Life was *Ivy Divey*, up and down.
If you gave a bad performance it was *Bruised*.

If you missed a cue or dropped a beat, he'd
Ring the bell on you to call you out.
He'd feel the heat of hate and say he felt
a draft and walk away. But when he hit you
with his silences, you'd know—a man who never
played an extra note or blew hard just
to blow, had walked away from *you*. And that's

enough,

that's cool.

3. Cutting the Hawk

Back in Kansas City at an all-night
jam: Colman Hawkins—still on tour with Fletcher
Henderson. Still called Bean, and still the King.
The Cherry Blossom Club on Vine St. Fake Buddha
on the stage keeping watch. Fake paintings
of Japan. All gold paint, burgundy satin. Dawn
is just a rumor stretching in beneath the door,
at most a feeling yet. Almost everyone had quit.
Coleman playing heavy, thick, and fast.

Calling out the hardest keys. Arpeggiating,
up and down a strut, his tempo swinging
Honeysuckle Rose and Sweet Lorraine to sleep
only to explode into a riff that hits them like a fist—

taking tunes they thought they knew out for
a stroll—roll them into dark rooms, fuck them silly
up against the alley walls, then bring them home.
Ok, your turn baby. But what's left? The song
rung out, exhausted, spent. The way he made
it wail and beg and plead, mouth working
on that reed as if it were a woman in a hurry.

The saxophone is not precise—no stable tone
or timbre. Breath vibrates through
a trembling slit into its throat and seeps out
spit from valves that press and pull on soft

pads, altering a thrum and hum, a bark. a shout
that gathers in the belly and comes rumbling
out the tunnel like a train or like air pushed
on up in front or like the hum of metal in your

hands. It all depends on how the player takes
that horn into the mouth, into the body, makes
of it a body. Imagine it like this. Coleman sweating
in a singlet, suspenders dangling. A strong man
straining, eyes shut tight, veins in the neck gone
taught. Then comes Lester, sweet, as if reaching
for the hand of that girl everyone has used, bullied,
pushed and pulled into their beds; and instead,
slides the chair out from the table. Rubs
the fingers in caress. Heavy-lidded eyes
that meet hers and make her laugh
a little, let her be the one who gets to say what
happens next. He dances in and then around
the phrase. So when the big man swings, he steps
into the place beneath, breezes in,
comes up close to plant a kiss and dance
away. Placing notes where no one

thought to play.

4. Playing with Billie

They thought *and* felt their way around a tune.
Piecing melodies apart. Play a single note, change
only timbre, tone and semitone. Purr a punctuated
pop, a pause, then blur it back into the verse.
His horn pitched at an angle tilted up, her head
tilted to the side as if in pain, his neck bent
down with slightest pressure on the reed,
the teeth, the lips. Carrying that horn as if it were
a lover that could hurt him and be hurt.

He followed her, she followed him deep into
the dim lights of the Zebra Room off Lenox,
1 a.m. Everybody hushed and close.
It hardly mattered who else played, who
was listening. Each tone fluid, rising up
the padded leather walls and out, flying broken-field,
a sparrow and a hawk, a sudden dive, a soaring
risk of drift and dying fall, embodying the vowel,
hollowing it out into half-empty streets, echoes
rising with the ghosts of garbagemen and junkies,
shoe-shine boys, jazzmen, dancers, singers, maids,
and whores, arching over instruments and tangled
sheets. Hurtling forward by holding off as if each
note were like a stone, a brick stretched back
at full arm's length, heavy, simmering with hunger,
hate and need and all the blinding windows

of 125th street. A quick breath like a gasp. A signal
to come slowly entering. Then Lester—quiet,
making her recall the rhythm and the song
she thought she'd sung: bending,
slurring, breathing all along its skin, pebbling
its surfaces, to waves that start to roll and crest
then blow back, inhale. She listens for the first
time once again—and the news is good

and terrible: how each love song has a riot
at its heart and the blues a healing bruise
you learn to find your courage in. She leans
into the spaces they have made, eyes closed
against her own reflection, shattering.

Billie Gets Strange

Black bodies hanging in the southern breeze
Strange fruit hanging from the poplar trees
—"Strange Fruit"

1.

Singing as theatrical display, the critics said,
trying to suggest she couldn't really sing.
Not like Ella, Dinah, Lena. Truth was, she
was *weird*. There's a reason only men could seem
to imitate that voice. It sounds approximate:
a steel encased in silk or is it the other way,
engaged and disengaged as if she played
the character in a tragedy about the life
of Billie Holiday. And the music was the score—
performance as mythology. Last song. Last set.
Her face in one pin spotlight in a silent room.
Café Society 1939. Disembodied, suspended
like the swaying bodies in the verse, in her voice,
hanging in a dead breeze thick with heat
she never lived or knew but did in phrase
on phrase that froze like breath, settled
like the weight of heavy fingers on the keys.

2.

And yet that fool who asked her, *sing that song*
again, the sexy one about the naked bodies
in the trees…had a point. She sang, uncanny,
like a cold sweat casting into swamps, like fever
and didn't turn away and didn't turn us *on* to agony, she
made us deal with just how sick we were
and are. Leather straps across the back but also buttocks
and the breasts. A pleasurable sting. She understood the lurid
and the lure. Body as fruit. Something to be swallowed
down, consumed, savored for the juice. A musk, a mask
that made it real—that sharp thrill we take in listening to
that song of death—in pain that we inflict as much as feel.

Beating the Shit Out of Billie Holiday

1.

He'd knock her down, stomp her loud enough
that they could hear it from the bandstand: slap
of skin, dull thud and thump. The band would try
to stall. Play a little heavy on the bass and drums.
As much to spare themselves as anyone. Hating
Levy, that fucking gangster. Minutes before the set
and he would show up, *Where's Billie? Gotta
beat her so she's in shape to sing.* And you
would have to point him toward the dressing
room. (Of course he knew where Billie was
he just wanted *you* to know and see if *you*
would try to stop him. You wouldn't). Imagine
what you do depends completely on another. Like
dancing if the dance could make its own melody
as it moved between two or three bodies floating
in and then back out again. Footfalls forming beats,
structure formed by how each dancer moved
and made their movements to each other.
Billie didn't have to move or even sing. Just
stand there and breathe. And if you played you
played for her and you at once and it was hers
and yours. And no one's. Love. Now imagine
you can hear that lover grunt and whimper
as you play a tune to drown her out.

2.

She said she wanted it, said she had to hurt
to sing at all and when her man kicked her
in the groin, that was good. *That was where
she sang from.* Crazy. But then she'd come,
pulsing from the dressing room, slow and sore
and radiant, shouting to her fans, *how you
doin baby?* They'd shout back *looking*

gorgeous Lady. She'd take a sip from every
glass on the table. Everyone would laugh.
A girl can hustle from the alley to the street
to the best club in the city. She still thinks
she has to pay for everything, especially
the gifts. And her gift was not a voice,
it was a source—a pulse. How do you
pay for that? How do you keep it? When
she rises slowly to the bandstand, waves
away the hands reached out to help, there is
a silence everywhere. Then the opening
bars, a blues. The lungs expand and *soon*
the opening of lips. And a singer and a song
begin to throb, blooming like a bruise.

Billie Shakes Free

1.

Now that I've told my story, / I'll take another shot of booze.
And if anyone should happen to ask you, / I've got those gamblers' blues
—St. James Infirmary Blues

No one knows exactly when she started.
They all sang, the girls who roared up and down
the pier, working sailors for those skinny
reefer cigarettes, working white boys down
from Jersey for their wallets. Blue Monday

on The Point—everybody balled. They would hit
the streets, sharp as razors. All the boys in pinstripes,
hats, and polished Florsheim shoes. And the girls
wearing anything and almost nothing. Eleanora
Fagan, 13 looking 22, a fast girl even then. Light-

skinned, big-breasted, over in the corner
of Ethel Moore's—just one voice and a record
spinning. Even then she'd bring the crowds
who followed her from club to bar
to good-time house. They all knew her. Hell,

they all knew everyone. But Eleanora topped
them all. Dancing, laughing, even the fucking
in the upstairs rooms would pause. To sing is to be

always copying a sound. Like how you learn to talk,
or like the birds do, you make your voice match
something—like a pitch, another voice, a cry, a moan.
Eleanora'd copy Louis Armstrong—St. James Infirmary
—not the voice. But the horn, the feel. The growl
that grooves and then begins to swing—heavy heavy
ball on a loooong chain rising up to hesitate, then

fall back again. Mimicry. But then she'd start in
doing her own thing *in-between* and just after, swing

the space *inside* a note or hold it back so long
you'd think your heart, your blood had stopped. It was
something—sweetness filthy clean and maybe just
a little terror in the joy to hear a girl that young, that free.

2.

Once upon a time before I started smiling
I hated the moonlight
—Blue Moon

Problem is, there are different kinds
of freedom—the kind you take, the kind you wish
that you could give away. No one gives it to you.
That's neglect. Eleanora, raped by a neighbor at ten,
then sent to a reformatory school for God and prayer,
then set loose again. That's the freedom of the stray. Sleep
in the warmest room and the room keeps changing

and is the same. You learn battle and hustle, beat
and take a beating. Come home late to the little place
on Spring Street. Or don't. Half-listen to your mamma
scream about what you can't do. No one
is your daddy. There are daddies everywhere. Bless
the child, sure. Find your own thing. Do it. But how much,
how far, and at what cost? Making it up as you go, but where to?

It's 1954 Carnegie Hall. Count Basie. Billie stumbling out
late to the stage as usual. The song is "Blue Moon"—she must
have sung it a thousand times in a thousand different rooms—
but she's just *gone.* And nothing sounds the same. Too many
strings, no space to step into. The sound a drowning thing.
They start in, she misses her cue, not late—*Lost.* They start

again. They stop. And she is on the docks in the cold; watching
the boats load and unload cargo. The whole bay creaks
with silence. Winter cold. Tuesday morning on The Point.
Still a little girl, a soft glow just beyond the bay
separates the sky from sea. To be unique is to be

alone and lost and, too often, hungry. They start again. *Blue Moon.*
Blue Moon, she thinks and sings *Shadows of the night*
That poets find beguiling / Seemed flat as the moonlight, and all
the boats at once pull against their moorings, reaching for the sea.

Notes

"Billie and the Art of Paraphrase." The title of this poem was suggested by the scholarly article, "Billie Holiday's Art of Paraphrase: A Study in Consistency" by Cynthia Folio and Robert W. Weisberg, Temple University Department of Psychology, in *New Musicology* (Poznan, Poland: Poznan Press, 2006, pp. 247-275), part of a series called Interdisciplinary Studies in Musicology. The song lyrics are from "All of Me" written by Gerald Marks and Seymore Simons.

"Billie Turns a Trick." Billie Holiday's words are quoted from Donald Clarke, *Billie Holiday: Wishing on the Moon* (Cambridge: Da Capo Press, 2000, p. 37). Because this was originally quoted from *Lady Sings the Blues,* it may be as much William Dufty's wording as it was Billie's. The quotation here has been slightly altered for rhythm and concision. The original is "With my regular white customers, it was a cinch. When they came to see me it was wham, bang, they gave me the money and were gone. I made all the loot I needed. But Negroes would keep you up all the damn night, handing you that stuff about 'Is it good, baby?' and 'Don't you want to be my old lady?'"

"Billie Holiday Doesn't Give a Fuck." Marie Bryant's words are quoted from Donald Clarke, *Billie Holiday: Wishing on the Moon* (Cambridge: Da Capo Press, 2000, p. 202). The song lyrics are from "Fine and Mellow" written by Billie Holiday.

"The Lady and the President." Jimmy Rowles' words are quoted from Donald Clarke, *Billie Holiday: Wishing on the Moon* (Cambridge: Da Capo Press, 2000, p. 126). The song lyrics are from "Billie's Blues" written by Billie Holiday. Lester Young's words are quoted from Donald Clarke, *Billie Holiday: Wishing on the Moon* (Cambridge: Da Capo Press, 2000, p. 128). The quotation here has been slightly altered for rhythm and concision. The original is "There's things going on up there, man. Some of you guys are all belly."

"Billie Gets Strange." Song Lyrics are from "Strange Fruit" written by Abel Meeropol (pseudonym: Lewis Allan).

"Beating the Shit out of Billie Holiday." Song Lyrics are from "My Man," originally titled "Mon Homme" by Jacques Charles, Channing Pollock, Albert Willemetz, and Maurice Yvain.

"Billie Shakes Free." Song lyrics are from "St. James Infirmary Blues," by J. Primrose and "Blue Moon" composed by Richard Rogers and Lorenz Hart.

Acknowledgments

"Billie Turns a Trick" first appeared in *The Connecticut River Review*.

All song lyrics used in the text are licensed and appear by permission. They are listed here in order appearance.

Book title, *Why Not Take All of Me*, from

ALL OF ME
Words and Music by Seymour Simons and Gerald Marks
©Copyright 1931 Marlong Music Corp (ASCAP), Round Hill Songs, Sony ATV/ Music Publishing LLC. All rights on behalf of Sony/ATV Music Publishing LLC, 8 Music Square West, Nashville, TN 37203. Used by permission. And Bienstock Publishing Company on behalf of Redwood Music Ltd. And Bourne Co. Copyright Renewed. All rights reserved. International Copyright Secured.

p. 11 "Why not take all of me" from

ALL OF ME
Words and Music by Seymour Simons and Gerald Marks
©Copyright 1931 Marlong Music Corp (ASCAP), Round Hill Songs, Sony ATV/Music Publishing LLC. All rights on behalf of Sony/ATV Music Publishing LLC, 8 Music Square West, Nashville, TN 37203. Used by permission. And Bienstock Publishing Company on behalf of Redwood Music Ltd. And Bourne Co. Copyright Renewed. All rights reserved. International Copyright Secured.

pp. 15-17 "My man he don't love me / Treats me ooh so mean," "Love will make you drink and gamble / Make you stay out all night long / Love will make you do things that you know is wrong," "He wears his high trimmed pants / stripes are really yellow / But when he starts to love me, he's so fine and mellow," and "Love is like a faucet / It turns off and on. / Sometimes when you think it's on. / It's turned off and gone" from

LOVER MAN
Written by Billie Holiday
Used by permission of Edward B. Marks Music Company

p. 18 "Some people say I'm built for speed" from

BILLIE'S BLUES
Written by Billie Holiday
Used by permission of Edward B. Marks Music Company

p. 24 "Black bodies hanging in the southern breeze / Strange fruit hanging from the poplar trees" from

STRANGE FRUIT
Words and Music by Lewis Allan ©Copyright 1939 (Renewed)
Used by permission of Edward B. Marks Music Company. And by Music
Sales Corporation (ASCAP). All Rights for the United States controlled by
Music Sales Corporation (ASCAP). International Copyright Secured.
All rights reserved.

p. 30 "Now that I've told my story, / I'll take another shot of booze. / And if anyone should happen to ask you, / I've got those gamblers' blues" from

ST. JAMES INFIRMARY
TRADITIONAL
Arranged by JOE PRIMROSE
© 1929 (Renewed) EMI MILLS MUSIC, INC.
Exclusive Print Rights Administered by
ALFRED MUSIC PUBLISHING CO., INC.
All Rights Reserved

pp. 30-31 "Once upon a time before I started smiling / I hated the moonlight" and "Shadows of the night / That poets find beguiling / Seemed flat as the moonlight" from

BLUE MOON
Music by RICHARD RODGERS
Lyrics by LORENZ HART
© 1934 (Renewed) METRO-GOLDWYN-MAYER INC.
All Rights (Excluding Print)
Controlled and Administered by EMI ROBBINS CATALOG INC.
Exclusive Print Rights Controlled and Administered by ALFRED MUSIC.
All Rights Reserved

About FutureCycle Press

FutureCycle Press is dedicated to publishing lasting English-language poetry and flash fiction books, chapbooks, and anthologies in both print-on-demand and ebook formats. Founded in 2007 by long-time independent editor/publishers and partners Diane Kistner and Robert S. King, the press incorporated as a nonprofit in 2012. A number of our editors are distinguished poets and writers in their own right, and we have been actively involved in the small press movement going back to the early seventies.

The FutureCycle Poetry Book Prize and honorarium is awarded annually for the best full-length volume of poetry we publish in a calendar year. Introduced in 2013, our Good Works projects are devoted to issues of universal significance, with all proceeds donated to a related worthy cause. Our Selected Poems series highlights contemporary poets with a substantial body of work to their credit. Our flash fiction line presents quick reads that can be serious or light-hearted, irreverent or quirky, fantastic or futuristic, or just plain fun.

We are dedicated to giving all of the authors we publish the care their work deserves, making our catalog of titles the most diverse and distinguished it can be, and paying forward any earnings to fund more great books.

We've learned a few things about independent publishing over the years. We've also evolved a unique, resilient publishing model that allows us to focus mainly on vetting and preserving for posterity the most books of exceptional quality without becoming overwhelmed with bookkeeping and mailing, fundraising activities, or taxing editorial and production "bubbles." To find out more about what we are doing, come see us at www.futurecycle.org.

www.ingramcontent.com/pod-product-compliance
Lightning Source LLC
Chambersburg PA
CBHW061201040426

42445CB00013B/1767